The abcs of Creating Your Children's Book

How to Write, Illustrate, Design,
Publish, and Market Your Picture Book

Gail M. Nelson

The ABCs of Creating Your Children's Book: How to Write, Illustrate, Design, Publish, and Market Your Picture Book

DESIGN/Books

ISBN 978-1-98-519753-4

Published by

e-book-design

Printed in the United States of America

Contents

Introduction

"Can a children's book change the world?"

~Linda Sue Park, author

My love affair with books began in childhood with story time. Every evening my three younger sisters and I would take a bath, put on our cozy flannel nightgowns, and choose a favorite book for Mom to read to us. We loved to share new adventures while poring over the colorful illustrations.

This love for books continues to feed my soul. It is a joy to be able to write and illustrate my own books, illustrate children's books written by other authors, and help writers of all genres self-publish their books.

But, can books really change the world? Studies have shown that books can inspire empathy, encourage smarter choices, and inform kids about the world. For example, the proceeds from Linda Sue Park's book, *A Long Walk to Water,* go toward building wells in South Sudan. Then, children, especially girls, can go to school—instead of carrying water for eight hours every day—which is life-changing!

10 Children's Books that Changed my Life

1 *Mrs. Piggle-Wiggle* by Betty MacDonald

2 *The Tale of Peter Rabbit* by Beatrix Potter

3 *Winnie-the-Pooh* by A. A. Milne and Ernest H. Shepard

4 *The Very Hungry Caterpillar* by Eric Carle

5 *Charlotte's Web* by E. B. White

6 *Harold and the Purple Crayon* by Crockett Johnson

7 *Guess How Much I Love You* by Sam McBratney

8 *The Paper Bag Princess* by Robert Munsch

9 *Goodnight Moon* by Margaret Wise Brown

10 *The Giving Tree* by Shel Silverstein

12 Steps to Creating Your Picture Book

1. Start with a really great idea.

2. Write in your own voice.

3. Read your story aloud— early and often.

4. Re-write based on feedback.

5. Edit manuscript professionally.

6. Balance words and pictures.

7. Illustrate professionally.

8. Choose where to publish.

9. Design interior and cover.

10. Proof thoroughly.

11. Publish your book.

12. Promote your book & yourself.

Does Self-Publishing Make Sense?

There are so many publishing options available to writers today, it's hard to know what is right for you. An author recently had her book accepted by a traditional publisher. Good news, right? Then she learned it would take two years before her book would be available, so she decided to publish it herself. She is 101 years old!

Independent authors can publish more quickly for a worldwide, online audience. Plus, there is more creative freedom to target smaller, niche markets. For example, if you search for a book topic that isn't available, it could be a great idea for your book.

If your heart is set on getting your book accepted by a traditional publisher, give yourself a time limit of perhaps a year or two, then consider self-publishing. However, if self-publishing already makes sense for your book project, read on!

Children's Book Author Tips

▷ Read a lot of children's books—classics, best sellers, and local authors.

▷ Join SCBWI (the Society of Children's Book Writers and Illustrators), www.scbwi.org.

▷ Take classes and workshops. Be open to learning and new ideas.

▷ Express your creativity. It's fun and you can make a difference.

▷ Network with children's book people, www.meetup.com.

▷ Read blogs on children's author websites. Start a blog or website.

▷ Do research on Amazon: best sellers in your category, descriptions, and reviews.

▷ Talk to librarians, book sellers, teachers, authors, and parents about your book ideas and topics.

Look for more tips in the following chapters.

Gail's Guidelines

Technical Tips

Write

"All of my books for young children have tremendous emotional content."

~Rosemary Wells, author & illustrator

Children do not like to be bored or preached to. If you can surprise them with tension, suspense, unpredictability, and fun, you will have a winning story. Keep the following in mind when writing for kids:

- Define your book hook. It should be simple, strong, and memorable. Search Amazon to find out if you have a unique niche in a specific children's book category.

- Write your back cover description early in the process to help clarify your book hook.

- Character development is essential. Your characters should show various emotions and moods through their interactions within the story.

- Choose active verbs in the present tense with no excess verbiage.

- Avoid lengthy descriptions. Show with illustrations; don't describe.

- Great picture books contain poetic elements and rhythmic language without a forced rhyming structure. Aim for a flowing rhythm with occasional rhyming words to improve readability.

Typical Word Counts

▷ 0 to 3 years old:
  under 100 words

▷ 3 to 7 years old:
  100 to 1,000 words

▷ 5 to 8 years old:
  under 2,000 words

Show or Tell—not both.

Write, edit, and set aside your manuscript for awhile. Come back to your story with "fresh eyes" and polish it. Then, read it aloud to as many people—and groups of children—as possible. Your text will become smoother and you'll get instant feedback from your audience.

When your story is as finished as you can make it, share it with some trusted beta readers (pre-readers) to get non-professional critiques. Rewrite any changes that make sense to you, and your manuscript will be ready for editing.

Hire a professional editor. Ask around in your personal network and get recommendations from other authors. Look for an editor with children's book experience, who relates to your book, and is a good fit for you. Children's books appear simple to edit; however, every word counts, making them very different from a novel or a nonfiction book.

Written Elements of a Great Picture Book

▷ Mood: Include emotions that are important to the story.

▷ Setting: Include a specific setting only if needed to complete the story.

▷ Details: Describe or show details, but not both.

▷ Flow: All content should add up to a coherent whole.

▷ Continuity: A linear timeline is important in children's books.

▷ Conclusion: Make sure the ending is consistent with the beginning.

The abcs of Creating Your Children's Book

Favorite Read Aloud Books

1. *Chicka Chicka Boom Boom* by Bill Martin Jr. & John Archambault
2. *Hop on Pop* by Dr. Seuss
3. *If You Give a Mouse a Cookie* by Laura Joffe Numeroff
4. *Brown Bear, Brown Bear, What Do You See?* by Bill Martin Jr. & Eric Carle
5. *Are You My Mother?* by P. D. Eastman
6. *Dear Zoo* by Rod Campbell
7. *Jamberry* by Bruce Degen
8. *First Tomato* by Rosemary Wells
9. *Goodnight iPad* by Ann Droyd
10. *The Little Mouse, The Red Ripe Strawberry, and the Big Hungry Bear* by Don Wood and Audrey Wood

Please note, there are three types of editors:

1. Developmental Editor: edits for flow, tone, pace, continuity, and structure. This type of editing should be done early in the process.

2. Copy Editor: edits for consistency of verb tense, voice, punctuation, and grammar.

3. Proofreader: fresh eyes to catch typos, inconsistencies, and details. This type of editing should be done after formatting has been completed.

Hosting for Author Websites & Blogs

- WordPress
- WIX
- Tumblr

Illustrate

"Children's picture book art is the
introduction to art for young people."

~Eric Carle, author and illustrator

Professional quality illustrations are a must for your book. If you are lucky enough to have the talent and training to create your own illustrations, congratulations! If not, seek out an artist or illustrator whose style fits what you visualize for your book.

You will want lively, action-packed pages with characters that have continuity from scene to scene, and throughout the book. The point of view should include different perspectives, like a television or movie director would produce. The goal of the illustrations is to depict your story with a unique look to help your book stand out.

Every great picture book has images that show playful, visual thinking. For example, a rabbit is the main character in Margaret Wise Brown's book *Goodnight Moon*, but a mouse appears on every two-page spread, adding an enjoyable hide-and-seek element to the content. Have fun imagining what the illustrations can add to your story.

10 Amazing Illustrators to Check Out

1. Eric Carle
2. Jon J. Muth
3. Jan Brett
4. Audrey Wood
5. Graeme Base
6. Jane Dyer
7. Chris Van Allsburg
8. Maurice Sendak
9. Lois Ehlert
10. Dr. Seuss

Visual Elements of a Great Picture Book

▷ Visual Clues: images show exactly what the text says and help young readers figure out the words and storyline.

▷ Action: show lively characters with continuity.

▷ Perspective or Point of View: the POV should vary from scene to scene, as in a TV show or movie.

▷ Add unrelated content: include surprise elements, such as hide-and-seek characters, to add interest.

▷ Goal: illuminate the story.

Whether or not you are an illustrator, it is a good idea to create a book dummy and/or a storyboard to help visualize your book. The standard vertical layout size is 8.5" wide by 11" tall, and a square layout is typically 8.5" x 8.5". (Horizontal is not recommended because of printer limitations.)

A storyboard or book dummy will show how the text and images work together, determine the page count, and fine-tune the flow of your story. You may find places that need notes to the illustrator to describe visual elements that are not in the text: the "show, don't tell" guideline.

This process will provide a guide to the format of each illustration—horizontal, vertical, or square—as well as the scale of each image on the page. It will show if the image "bleeds" off the edge, or floats within the text. And, it will help you avoid placing anything important in the gutter.

The abcs of Creating Your Children's Book

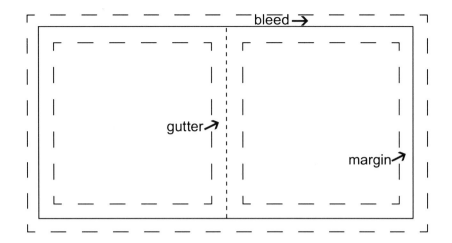

Next, proceed to rough sketches, final sketches, then finished art work, which should be created "to scale."

Original art will need to be scanned or photographed to convert to a digital format for printing. Scans or digitally created images should be saved as JPGs at 300 dpi.

If you plan to work with a freelance illustrator, start by asking for a sample illustration from more than one person to get a feel for their style and how they work. Communication will be the key to a successful collaboration.

Typical Page Counts

▷ 0 to 3 years old: 20-24 pages

▷ 3 to 7 years old: 32 pages

▷ 8 years old and up: 40 pages and up

Freelance Illustrators

• fiverr.com
• freelancer.com
• Upwork.com

Storyboard Template

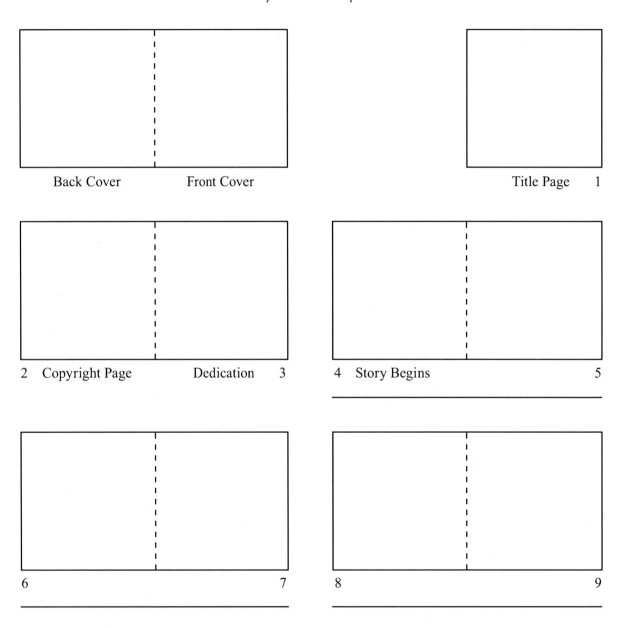

Back Cover   Front Cover

Title Page   1

2   Copyright Page   Dedication   3

4   Story Begins   5

6   7

8   9

The abcs of Creating Your Children's Book

How to Illustrate a Picture Book

1. Draw thumbnails to work out the composition. Show a consistent style.

2. Research your subject matter. Drawing something you don't know well shows insecurity and looks unprofessional.

3. Draw full-size illustrations on tracing paper to transfer to art paper— don't erase on your good paper.

4. Always use quality materials.

5. Try different brands and types of paper for different techniques.

6. Experiment with various mediums.

7. Create practice pieces to test paper, medium, and color palette.

8. Start over if needed. Don't overwork a piece.

9. Always do your best. Take the time to make it right.

10. Do professional quality work—neatness counts!

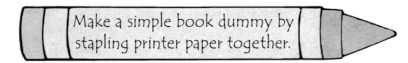

Make a simple book dummy by stapling printer paper together.

Design

"There are three responses to a
piece of design—yes, no, and WOW!"

~Milton Glaser, graphic designer and children's book illustrator

The layout and design of your book is the digital formatting that will provide the print-ready files for publication. There will be two separate files: one for the cover and one for the interior.

A freelance book designer can be hired, or you can use a layout program, such as KindleCreate (free from Amazon) or Adobe InDesign. InDesign is available through Adobe.com for a monthly fee, with discounts for teachers and students. Tutorials are available online but, keep in mind, it will take quite a time commitment to learn to use such a complex program.

Freelance Designers

- fiverr.com
- freelancer.com
- Upwork.com

Design Choices to Make

▷ Paperback or hardcover (Hardcovers are available through independent printers.)

▷ Cover: images and fonts.

▷ Cover finish: matte or glossy.

▷ Interior: font and font size.

▷ Interior: margins, columns, bleeds, and image placement.

▷ Interior: location of page numbers (if included.)

▷ Illustrations: the medium and color or grayscale.

▷ Paper: white or cream is available for black and white books; and only white paper with color images.

Design Checklist

Cover:

☐ Title

☐ Author name

☐ Illustrator name (if different)

☐ Back cover description

☐ Price (optional)

☐ ISBN / barcode

Interior—Front Matter:

☐ Title page

☐ Copyright page,
   with ISBN

☐ Dedication page

Interior—Back Matter:

☐ About the Author,
   with photo

☐ About the Illustrator,
   with photo

An eye-catching cover design is key to the success of your book. The cover must ensure that the title can be easily read in a thumbnail size during online browsing. Images on the cover should intrigue readers. Colors should enhance concepts and emotions found in the book. And, fonts should be chosen to reinforce a theme, while being easy to read.

It would be a very worthwhile investment to hire a professional book cover designer, if your budget allows. However, if you decide to create your own cover, start by researching your category on Amazon. Keep in mind that interior illustrations can be repurposed for the cover. Stock images may also be considered for your book cover (and interior.) Free and low-cost stock photos and clip art can be found online. Be sure to follow all copyright regulations that apply.

Look up the print specifications on Kindle Direct Publishing for guidelines to the layout of the back cover, spine, and front cover. (The

The abcs of Creating Your Children's Book

width of the spine is calculated by multiplying the page count by the thickness of the paper.)

NOTE: Leave space in the lower right corner of the back cover for the barcode.

Send proofs of a few cover designs to your beta readers. Ask them to vote for their favorite cover and get feedback on what they like or dislike about each design. Incorporate suggestions into your final design and export a print-ready PDF.

The interior design of your book must also meet printer specifications. Set guidelines for the margins, bleed, gutter, etc. Be aware of the importance of white space. Choose a font that is easy to read. Some fonts have an "elementary a"—the "a" children are taught to write in school. (For example: Futura—a, Kids—a, Segoe Print—a.) Print and proof the interior pages.

NOTE: The ISBN will need to be added to the copyright page after it has been assigned, then export the print-ready PDF.

Choosing a Freelance Designer

1. Read online reviews of their work.
2. View samples online or pay for a custom sample.
3. Communicate clearly and effectively.

Stock Images

- dreamstime.com
- free-graphics.com
- free-clip-art.com

A great kid's book appeals to both children and adults.

Publish

"The publishing of a book is a worldwide event."

~Salman Rushdie

As an independent author, you may choose to have your book printed and published where you like. It is wonderful to have this creative freedom, and an independent printer may be a good option, such as for hardcover books.

I have found that the simplest way to publish your book is through Kindle Direct Publishing on Amazon. Advantages include: a free Amazon listing, a free ISBN, an author page, high-quality printed books at member prices, and worldwide distribution with connections to outlets you would not normally reach. Approximately 60% of all book sales are now through Amazon so your book will have a marketing advantage from the start. Plus, it's easy! Step by step guidelines on the following page will simplify the process of publishing your children's book.

My First Children's Book

I created my first picture book after a visit to the zoo with my daughter. Together, we wrote a story about the zoo animals gobbling up healthy foods, while a puppy munches on junk food until he runs out of energy to play. I wanted to show children how to make healthier food choices—my daughter was just having fun!

Go Eat, Pete was published through an independent publishing company, which provided locally printed books that I sold at schools and libraries. A few years later, I published the second edition through Kindle Direct Publishing on Amazon, which provides passive income and has led to greater satisfaction and success.

10 Steps to Publishing on Kindle Direct Publishing

1. Open an account on KDP.com. Fill in the publishing, payment, and tax information for your account.

2. Start your new book project: enter your book title, choose Paperback, and get started with the guided setup.

3. Fill in the following information: subtitle (if needed), primary author (you), contributors (for example, illustrator, if different than the author), and click on the Save & Continue button.

4. Assign an ISBN (International Standard Book Number). The free KDP-assigned ISBN will give you the best distribution options.

5. Add the ISBN-13 to your copyright page and export the interior to PDF.

6. Choose the interior layout type and size. Upload your book's interior print-ready PDF file. Click Save.

7. Choose a matte or glossy book cover finish and upload the print-ready PDF cover file. Save. Kindle Direct Publishing will add the barcode to the lower right corner of the back cover.

8. Submit files for review. You will receive an email within 24 hours.

9. Review the digital proof. Make changes, if needed, and re-upload the PDF.

10. Order a printed proof of your book for final proofreading.

Next Steps

While waiting for the file review, fill in the Description information on Kindle Direct Publishing. You should already have a description from the writing step that can be copied and pasted into the description window.

Next, choose a Category that best fits the subject matter of your book. Add additional information as needed. Then, enter five Keywords or phrases, separated by commas, that readers would use to search for your book on Amazon. Click the Save button.

After your file review has been approved, order a printed proof of your book. While waiting for it to arrive, check out the Sales & Marketing link on Kindle Direct Publishing for promotional activities you can begin.

Review your book proof carefully after it arrives and make any necessary changes. Upload the revised PDF and approve the proof for publication. Congratulations! You are now a published author.

Alternative Publishing Formats

▷ Hardcover books: available at independent printers

▷ Apps: TaleSpring.com or hire a freelance app developer

▷ eBooks for iTunes and Barnes and Noble: Smashwords.com

▷ eBooks for Amazon: KDP.com (Kindle Direct Publishing)

▷ eBooks with Audible Narration: ACX.com through Amazon

Research Keywords

• amazon.com
• keyword tool.io
• ubersuggest.org

Market

"There is always a market for AWESOME."

~Jennifer Laughran, literary agent

Start Marketing Before your Book is Done

▷ Build your author website and brand.

▷ Start collecting an email list by offering free online gifts, such as coloring pages or activity sheets, to grow your fan base.

▷ Start blogging about your book's topic (not your book.)

▷ Guest blog on popular sites.

▷ Open a Twitter account.

▷ Join Pinterest and create posts about your book's topic.

▷ Join Goodreads and open an author account.

▷ Create a Facebook page and join or start a group.

Authors can make connections with their readers in many different ways: high tech or low tech, digital or print. Try a few ideas in this chapter to see which approach best fits your personality and sense of community.

You may want to have some promotional print materials designed and printed, such as business cards, bookmarks, post cards, a poster of your book cover, a banner, t-shirts, games, and/or magnets.

Another option is to try online marketing, such as email announcements, Facebook ads, Pinterest posts, YouTube videos, podcasts, blogs, tweets, or texts.

A creative approach would be to wear a name tag that says, "Ask me about my new book!" at a networking event. Or, consider entering a few book contests to get some exposure and spread the word about your book. Also, honest, professional reviews are available through Kirkus and Blue Ink Review for nominal fees.

Marketing Steps After your Book is Published

▷ Open your Author Central account on Amazon.

▷ Ask beta readers and friends for reviews on Amazon.

▷ Host a book launch party and plan celebrations with other authors.

▷ Offer to do read-alouds at schools, libraries, or coffee shops.

▷ Post photos from your outings on social media.

▷ Add your book to your email signature.

▷ Find reviewers on Facebook and add author apps to your FB page.

▷ Sell your books in local gift shops, coffee shops, and book stores.

▷ Create a video book trailer on Animoto and post it to YouTube.

▷ Ask friends to request your book at the library.

▷ Share a book with your doctor's or dentist's office for exposure.

▷ Create a press release and submit it online and to local newspapers.

▷ Offer your book for fundraising events or donate a portion of sales to a charity.

▷ Create a one-sheet/sell sheet to help pitch your book.

▷ Always have your books on hand.

In conclusion, marketing can be the most challenging piece of the children's book publishing puzzle. Try new things on a regular basis to make it fun and interesting. Keep in mind that marketing is a marathon, not a sprint. Be persistent and your book can continue to sell for many years.

Marketing Websites

- authorcentral. amazon.com
- goodreads. com/author. program

One-sheet Template

Book Cover	Book Title
	Subtitle
	Tagline

Author Photo

A short synopsis about the book, similar to the back cover description. Leave readers wanting more.

~~~~~

Author Name
Illustrator Name
Publishing Company
ISBN
Publication Date
Size
Page count
Category
List Price
Distributor

Testimonials, with names.

~~~~~

About the Author

A short, memorable biography.

Bookmarks and coloring pages are fun marketing tools.

Resources

"Do what you love and the necessary resources will follow."

~Peter McWilliams

Books

From Pictures to Words: A Book about Making a Book by Janet Stevens

Writing with Pictures: How to Write and Illustrate Children's Books by Uri Schulevitz

Children's Writer's & Illustrator's Market, publishing guide— updated yearly

How to Write and Illustrate Children's Books and Get Them Published, Consultant Editors: Treld Pelkey Bicknell and Felicity Trotman

The Encyclopedia of Writing and Illustrating Children's Books by Desdemona McCannon, Sue Thornton, and Yadzia Williams

Buzz: Your Super Sticky Book Marketing Plan by Polly Letofsky

Websites

Underdown.org: self-publishing information

SCBWI.org: Society of Children's Book Writing and Illustrating

NWP.org: National Writing Project

KDP.com: paperbacks and ebooks on Amazon

Smashwords.com: ebooks on iTunes, Barnes and Noble, etc.

bisg.org/page/bisacedition: subject headings list

PerryMarshall.com/grade: grade level score of text

SteubenPress.com: hardcover books and printed marketing materials

MyWordPublishing.com: book coach and self-publishing help

About the Author

Little Me

Gail M. Nelson is passionate about books. She loves to design books, illustrate picture books, and read for her many book clubs. Gail graduated with a Master's degree in fine art, and she has been a freelance artist, illustrator, and graphic designer for over thirty years. Gail makes her home in the mountains of Colorado with her husband, dog, garden, the deer and the hummingbirds.

Made in United States
North Haven, CT
27 February 2023

33285773R00020